A Special Gift

Presented to:

....

From:

....

Date:

....

stories, sayings, and scriptures to Encourage and Inspire

hugs
for
the
hurting

HOWARD
PUBLISHING CO.

West Monroe, Louisiana

Our purpose at Howard Publishing is to:

- *Increase faith* in the hearts of growing Christians
- *Inspire holiness* in the lives of believers
- *Instill hope* in the hearts of struggling people everywhere

Because He's coming again!

Hugs for the Hurting
© 1997 by Howard Publishing Co., Inc.
All rights reserved

Published by Howard Publishing Co., Inc.,
3117 North 7th Street, West Monroe, LA 71291-2227

Printed in the United States of America

05 06 07 08 09 10   25 24 23 22 21

Stories by John William Smith, author of *My Mother's Favorite Song, My Mother Played the Piano,* and contributor to other *Hugs* books

Scriptures paraphrased by LeAnn Weiss, owner of Encouragement Company, Orlando, Florida

Jacket Design and Interior Art by LinDee Loveland
Edited by Philis Boultinghouse

The previous printing was catalogued as follows:

Library of Congress Cataloging-in-Publication Data

Hugs for the heart for the hurting : stories, sayings, and scriptures to encourage and inspire.
     p. cm.
    ISBN 1-878990-68-3 (alk. paper)
    1. Christian life. I. Howard Publishing Co.
BV4501.2.H813 1997
242—dc21

97-682
CIP

contents

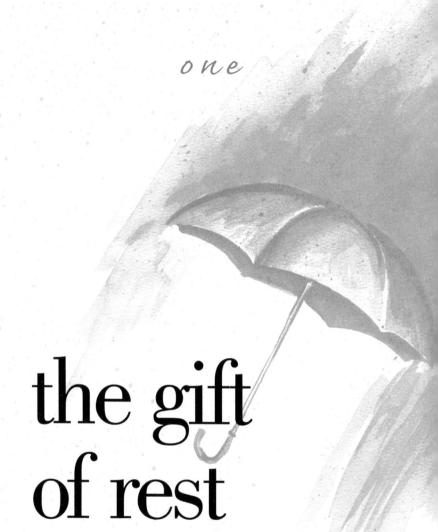

the gift
of rest

*L*ife can be tiring and frustrating at times! Come to me when you are worn down – stressed out with circumstances and burdens that are weighing you down. I will give you rest!

Love,

Your God of Peace and Rest

Matthew 11:28–30
John 10:10

Do you ever feel that your life is a horrible nightmare? Do you sometimes wish you could just wake up and it would all go away?

When the haze of hurting moves in and threatens to shut out all the light in your life, it's time to gaze at the eternal light far off in the distance. This inviting light offers comfort in times of trouble, peace in the place of pain, and an enduring hope that no darkness can smother. This light is the light of home – your real home. It's the light of heaven. When life becomes a bad dream, close your eyes and take a little mind trip to heaven – it's a wonderful place to visit.

In the last weeks of Christ's life, when the ominous darkness of betrayal and death hovered over him and his disciples, he comforted his confused followers with thoughts of heaven: "Don't let your hearts be troubled. Trust in God; trust also in me. In my Father's house are many rooms . . ."

Can you picture it? The fresh fragrance of new construction fills the place. Excitement and anticipation pervade the air. Each room and every hallway is lit up with the warm love of the living God. No fear lurks in the darkness, because there is no darkness. And listen, do you hear the music? It's the joyful sound of the angels' songs. You can't help but join their chorus.

You approach a doorway where Jesus is standing. With one nail-scarred hand he points to a golden nameplate, and with the other he touches your shoulder. The nameplate bears your name; his gentle voice speaks words of assurance, "Take heart. I have overcome the world and all of its pain. One day you will be with me in this place, and all that you are going through now will seem only a bad dream. Until then, feel free to visit here in your heart any time you wish. And by the way, you can invite as many as you can to come with you. There's plenty of room."

The little troubles and worries of life, so many of which we meet, may be as stumbling blocks in our way, or we may make them stepping stones to a noble character and to heaven.

—Henry Ward Beecher

Life was born again by the morning – I tingled with it – I wanted to open the window and shake my fist at The Nameless Dread and say, "I beat you."

the nameless dread

"As the sun was setting,
Abram fell into a deep sleep,
and a thick and dreadful darkness
came over him."
—Genesis 15:12

When I was a child, I had a recurring bad dream. In my dream I was standing on a vast, flat, endless, unbroken, grassy plain. There were no large rocks, valleys, hills, trees, water, people, or towns – not a single place to hide or seek shelter. I had no idea how I got to this place – it was as though I had been suddenly born there. As I looked about me, I was filled with a sense of dread – as though I were in danger from some as yet unknown source. I slowly became aware of something like a vast cloud bank that stretched from earth to sky and from one edge of the horizon to the other. It moved slowly but purposefully in my direction,

the gift of rest

becoming darker and more ominous with each moment. It was –

The Nameless Dread!

I do not know how it got that title – it was not of my doing. I only know that from the first time I saw it, I knew that –

that was its name.

My reaction was always the same. I would begin to run – to seek any kind of shelter. I ran slowly at first, casting my eyes frantically about me, sure that there *must* be – *had* to be – some nook that I had overlooked. Finding nothing, I would increase my pace as the dark horror drew nearer. Ultimately, I would find myself running in abject terror as fast as I could until I was totally exhausted – until my breath came in ragged gasps – until my legs simply would no longer move at my bidding. I would scream for help, but my screams could only be heard in my head – never in my ears – and I was aware that in this land, there was no sound, because there was no one to hear. The sound went out, but it never came back.

the nameless dread

I was alone.
Alone in a way that I had never known –
alone with
The Nameless Dread.

The creeping darkness was cruelly relentless. It never hurried, changed its pace, or varied its direction. It was absolutely sure of its quarry. Actually, The Nameless Dread wasn't after me – I mean, personally and individually. I was nothing to it – no more than a stone or blade of grass – it simply moved across this plain every day, consuming everything in its path.

At the end of my dream, when I had reached the last extremity of my strength, I would fall to my knees, interlock my fingers, and raise my hands in a supplicating posture and beg for mercy. I would cry and plead for clemency in the most touching, sympathetic, and endearing terms. The Nameless Dread never responded. It did not and could not hear. It never altered its countenance –

it simply came on.

Just as it reached me – just as I was about to be enveloped and overwhelmed by its misty blackness,

the gift of rest

which I always interpreted as death, I awoke. My first waking sensation was always the vague awareness of light. I would gradually, fearfully open my eyes – assuming that I was dead and wondering what kind of world I was waking to – and the light would grow. Familiar things – the quilt, the picture on the wall, my chest of drawers – came into view. I would look out the window and there would be the chicken coop – right where it ought to be – the well and the pump, the outhouse, the pear tree, and then, down below the house, the misty fog rising from the swamp. I was alive! It had only been a dream.

"Oh God," I would say, "Oh God,
it was just a dream –
it was just a dream –
it was just a dream!"

Over and over I would repeat that phrase as the wonderful, dawning reality swept over me that I was not dead – that I was not awakening to a new and frightening world. I would be drenched with sweat, trembling from head to foot; real tears would streak my face, and my fingers would ache from being clenched for so long. Gradually, I would begin to relax, pulling the familiar quilt up around my chin – its realness assuring me – as the glory of being alive – of living – washed over me.

You cannot imagine the pleasure I took in the simplest things. I would slowly finger my old, worn blanket – made for me by my grandma Smith – tracing the quilted pattern as though I were seeing it for the first time. The chicken coop and the outhouse were not the drab, decaying, ordinary things they had been. They were wonderful, glorious structures – and I took individual pleasure in them. The smells from our kitchen would float into my room, and they were not of ham and eggs but of exotic dishes – ambrosia and the nectar of the gods. All of these things were created anew for me every time I had the dream. Life was born again by the morning – I tingled with it – I wanted to open the window and shake my fist at

The Nameless Dread
and say,
"I beat you."

the gift of rest

All of us at times feel the creeping, overwhelming, blackness of The Nameless Dread. It has many names and many faces, and it comes in many forms. We call it aging or loneliness or cancer. We call it fear, heartache, hopelessness, ingratitude, guilt, death, or depression. And when it enters our lives, we run before it, frantically seeking shelter, vainly seeking help.

And finally, we reach the last extremity of our strength, and we fall to our knees, begging for clemency – and we lift our eyes to heaven – and we see standing there the Son of Man, with arms outstretched, with hope upheld. He's standing where he's always been – waiting for us to look up – waiting for us to seek his aid. For the child of God, the blackness of The Nameless Dread is overcome

by the light of the Son.

Deliverance from The Nameless Dread does not necessarily mean deliverance from its earthly forms – for we are not promised relief from aging, from heartache, from sickness, or from death – but we are promised relief from the hopelessness of it all, relief from the feelings of powerlessness, relief from the dread of it all. For the child of God, there is hope and joy even in the midst of pain.

And even greater than the relief we find here is the absolute relief on the other side of the sleep of death. For when the children of God awake, the next sensation will be of light. We will open our eyes to familiar objects and familiar faces. "Yes," we'll say, "there is the pear tree and there is the chicken coop and there are my loved ones – Jary, Priscilla, Mom and Dad, Judi, Lincoln, Amy, Brendan, Kamber, Kristen, and Debbie. And there is the Holy City – just as John described it and more glorious than I ever imagined it." The alabaster walls reach ever higher, and at the twelve gates, each made of a single pearl, stands a herald to welcome home the children of God. The city stands sparkling in brilliant light – but it's not the sun – this light is a truer, cleaner, whiter, and clearer than ever the sun knew. There are no shadows here, for the light is everywhere – it is the light of presence – of being – of God's own face beaming in the glorious victory of His Son.

"Oh God," we will say, "Oh God" – and it won't be a word of hope but of reality.

the gift of rest

"Oh God, it was just a dream,
it was just a dream,
and now I am alive –
more alive than I have ever been –
and I shall never sleep again
and never dream again
and never, never again fear –
The Nameless Dread."

reflections . . . .

two

the gift
of life

You can soar even in storms because I strengthen you! Remember, you can do all things through me!

Love,

Your Father of Every Good

and Perfect Gift

P.S. I have given you everything you need for life and godliness.

Philippians 4:13

2 Peter 1:3

You have been given a gift. This gift is not wrapped in tissue paper or tied with a beautiful bow, but it has been prepared with the greatest of care by the Master Gift Giver. Priceless in nature, no gift in all the world is more sought after than this – it is the gift of life – your life.

And yet, even before this gift was yours, it was tainted by the schemes of the Spoiler – for his intent is to spoil all that's good. He sends rains of sorrow and floods of defeat, but the Gift Giver will not have his purposes thwarted. For through the storms of life, the Savior's voice is heard more clearly than before, and his presence is felt with intense reality. Through the blinding rain, the Life Giver extends his nail-scarred hand and takes your trembling hand firmly in his own.

With our hands safe in his, we borrow what we need from him. He lends us his courage and strength, and paths that we thought were impassable pass beneath our feet, and we move with him beyond the storm. And there, in the gleaming light of day, we see the eternal value of our lives and know that the gift of life here on earth is made even more valuable by virtue of the chastening of the storm.

Your life is a gift.

God may be invisible, but He's in touch. You may not be able to see Him, but He is in control. And that includes what you just lost. That includes what you've just gained. That includes all of life—past, present, future.

—Charles Swindoll

"Just follow me, and do what I do. I always save a little for the end – for this last hill – you can borrow from me."

the life of
susan edgin

She was the older sister of my son's wife, and her name was Susan. She was a nice girl – a good girl. She was *good* in the traditional sense that she loved her family, her friends, her dog, obeyed her parents, studied hard, slept late, was kind and thoughtful of others, sang in the church choir, cleaned up her messes, made good moral decisions, loved God, was silly, laughed a lot, cried some, and all in all, was the kind of daughter that every parent dreams of having. She loved life and lived it to the fullest every waking moment. She took good care of her body, watched what she ate, exercised regularly, was neat in her appearance, and went to great pains with her hair and clothes.

the gift of life

I think that at first glance she would be judged as no more than average-pretty, but if you looked deeply into those large, luminous, all-telling eyes or listened attentively to that intriguing, animated voice, it would soon occur to you that she was quite beautiful. She was a tall girl, lithe, athletic, and graceful in all her movements. She carried herself well – with dignity, style, and verve. She never took herself too seriously, but she was thoughtful enough to be introspective when the occasion called for it. She was a loyal friend, a great lover of children and the simple things of life, and she sang beautifully.

I know you think that I am just romanticizing, but I'm not. My son put it this way: "If you went anywhere I have ever lived, you would find someone who didn't like me, but that wasn't true of Susan. I never met or heard of anyone who didn't like Susan Edgin."

For the short time I knew her, we spent a fair amount of time together. Susan was so refreshingly open that you didn't need to be around her long to feel that you were her best friend.

Once, when I was staying at her house, we went running together. She thoughtfully adjusted her pace to accommodate my aging legs. Susan talked the whole way. (I am tempted to make a pun and say she kept up a *running conversation*, but I won't.) I don't talk when I run. It isn't that I am concentrating or unfriendly; it's that talking requires breath and energy, and I don't have any to spare when I'm running. After about four miles, I was nearing exhaustion. We came at last to the bottom of the long, steep hill that led to her house.

As we approached the incline I said, "Susan, I just can't make it, you go ahead."

"Sure you can," she said, "just follow me, and do what I do. I always save a little for the end – for this last hill – you can borrow from me."

I followed her.
I did what she did,
and I borrowed a little
of what she had saved
for the end.

When we got to the top, she turned and laughed and said, "See there, you can always do a little more than you think –

especially if you have someone with you."

the gift of life

Susan's gone now. She died on May 19, 1995, in an automobile accident near Augusta, Georgia. The car she was traveling in spun out of control on a wet road and slammed sideways into a guard rail. Susan was crushed. In the short time she lived after the accident, calls went out for prayers. We poured out our hearts to God in agony, begging him to save her. The doctors tried everything that medical science could do, but she died.

It doesn't seem fair, you know. Here I am still plodding up hills, and I'm thirty-five years older than Susan – it doesn't seem right. You can't help the nagging doubts; they are an integral part of a growing faith. I started asking those questions a long time ago. The only answer I've found is to trust God. It hasn't been easy, and I still ask the questions, but I know that I don't have a clue – so I trust him.

What is life?

I think I know. Life is a gift – a precious, beautiful, gift. Yes, that is exactly what life is. It is something to hold – but not too closely – because it isn't ours. That is why Jesus instructed Mary not to hang on to him.

the life of susan edgin

God gave Susan to us for twenty-seven years, and he let us know her and love her and bask in the glow of her vitality – but *she was never ours.* That is the great mistake we make. We become so used to things that we begin thinking that they're ours. That's what leads us into asking stupid questions about justice and fairness and –

"What if . . . ?"

Life originates with God. Even our personal lives are not our own. Life has nothing to do with fairness, and its value or justification cannot be measured by longevity. It is not sad to die young. What is sad is to die and never to have lived, to have been alive and never to have seen anything or known God. We don't feel that kind of sadness for Susan. Susan lived a full life because she saw the created world through eyes of faith and because she knew the God who made it.

Susan was a gift – and the only proper response to a gift – is gratitude.

"Thank you,
O Lord of the Universe,
for Susan."

the gift of life

I honestly don't remember the last time I saw her or what we said. We didn't try to make it important because we thought we'd see each other again – soon and often. I guess it really wasn't too important, because we will see each other again – soon and often – and we'll pick up right where we left off.

Susan has climbed her last hill – it was a long, steep grade – even for young legs, and she didn't know if she could make it, but when she started the ascent, she found Jesus beside her, and he said –

"Just follow me, and do what I do.
I always save something for the end –
for this last hill –
you can borrow from me."

And so she followed Jesus, and she did what he did, and she borrowed some of what he had saved, and they climbed the hill together and passed over to the other side. And it's true, you know –

it is easier,
if you have someone with you.

Life is a gift.

reflections . . . .

the gift of healing

Your flesh and your heart may fail. But, remember . . . I am the strength of your heart and your destiny *forever!*

Love,

Your God of Healing and Restoration

Psalm 73:26

Our God is a God of healing. He is a mender, a fixer of broken things. And we need such a God, because we tend to break and spoil much of what we touch. When we allow him to come into our fretful hearts, he works quietly and gently; and with the skill of a tender craftsman, he begins the work of restoring what is lost.

You won't feel his every move, but one day you'll sense a change – a change that stirs within you the desire to right a wrong. Perhaps you'll be moved to write a letter to a friend or relative who has been distanced by

anger or bitterness. Perhaps you'll think
of calling a cherished loved one whom you
hurt with careless words.

Go on, make the move. You'll find that God
has already prepared the path to restored love. It
may not be easy at first – mending broken hearts
never is – but the Miracle-Maker has already
applied his providence and touched the heart
awaiting your move.

Always be in a state
of expectancy, and
see that you leave
room for God to
come in as He likes.

—Oswald Chambers

For the first time in
a long time, he had
a plan – he knew
exactly what he was
doing and why.

going home

If you had asked him why he came back, he would have said that quite honestly, he didn't know. He had been born here and had graduated from high school here and married here. He had grown up in this town. He had played football here and, after four years of college, had returned to marry his high school sweetheart. He hadn't been back in years. It wasn't that he had no good memories. It was that

the latest and most dominant were bad.

Lately, he had just felt a great wrongness in his life. An undefined anxiety – depression – heaviness. He found himself sitting at his desk drumming his fingers and staring vacantly at reports wondering why they were important. Sometimes he turned the nameplate that sat on the front of his desk around and stared at his name – "George Franklin," he said. "Who is George Franklin?" He gazed long moments out his office window at the windows in other office buildings, wondering who worked over there and what they were like. He wondered what they thought about and if they ever looked at his window and wondered about him. He also noticed, with some alarm, that he was having trouble making even the most simple decisions.

He knew he was lonely, but this maddening, haunting feeling that nothing seemed to shake was more than loneliness – it was like the instinct that drives a wounded animal to its den. He felt the need to *get somewhere* – someplace where he could find his center again, his foundation – his *home*. Yes, that was exactly what he wanted, and that was why he had come back to this town – it was the closest thing to home he had ever known.

This primitive instinct drives many thoughtful people – it drives some to drink, some to drugs, some to work harder, some to power, some to affairs, some to church, some to diets, travel, poetry, mysticism, fitness centers, sporting events, TV, or cheap novels.

It drove him
home.

going home

When he drove into town, he was very disappointed. Much was gone; much more had changed. He didn't recognize anyone. Now that he was here, he didn't know what to do. He had thought that just coming back would provide the reason – it didn't. He drove around a little – went by the high school, looking for old, familiar landmarks. He stopped in a restaurant for a cup of coffee and finally recognized an old acquaintance. They shook hands, exchanged pleasantries, and bragged a little on what they had accomplished. "How's Alice?" Pete asked. It was an inevitable question, but it was the one he wanted to avoid most of all. "She's fine, I guess. I suppose you haven't heard that we're separated. I haven't seen her in nearly two years."

"Separated! No kidding! Gee, everybody thought you were Mr. and Mrs. ideal couple. Two years! Why don't you just get a divorce?"

He had wondered the same thing – many times. He wondered why she hadn't forced the issue – demanded one. He mumbled some nonsense about the financial difficulty of the settlement; and of course, they couldn't agree about the kids – but there was something else, something more – something never put into words, but he knew what it was. Divorce was too *final – the end –* and neither of them had the courage or the heart to say that it was finally and forever over. That would close the book on too many things they wanted to keep.

Pete was in the real estate business, and finally George asked him if he remembered the house they had lived in. "Sure," Pete said. "In fact, I've got it listed." Without really thinking about it, George said, "Let's drive by; I'd like to see what they've done to the old place."

His mind flooded with memories as they drove down the familiar street – maybe he had been happier here than he thought. Pete had a key to the lockbox, and very shortly, George found himself wandering through the empty rooms. "This is it," he said to himself; "this is why I came back."

And he knew that was the truth.

The grass had not been cut in back. The previous owners had not cared properly for the grapes or the fruit trees; the bedrooms needed paint badly. "You know," he thought, "I always meant to pipe the water from the washing machine out to the trees, and I think

going home

Alice was right about putting a mantle over the fire-place. In fact, now that Scott is bigger, we could finish that back room, put in another bath, and have a bedroom to ourselves."

It began to dawn upon him – very slowly – what a good time he was having, how excited he was, that he was planning in terms of *we* instead of *I* – and that gave meaning to the future. But his excitement vanished as he realized that it was all a myth, a cruel unreality. It struck him forcefully that he didn't own this house, he didn't live in this town, he had no job here, and of course, Alice and the kids lived far away. But the idea wouldn't leave him, and he knew – just as a homing pigeon knows – that he was home and that *this was his one chance* and that

he had to try.

"How much are they asking, Pete?"

"Seventy-five thousand, but they'll take sixty-eight."

"I'll take it." George couldn't believe it was his voice that he heard. There was assurance in it. For the first time in a long time, *he had a plan* – he knew exactly what he was doing and why. "I'll call her," he thought;

the gift of healing

"I'll call her tonight." But he couldn't wait for tonight, so he called her at work. Normally he asked for "Alice," but today he asked for "Mrs. George Franklin." He heard the secretary whisper, "Alice, it's for you, some guy wants to speak to *Mrs. George Franklin.*" When she picked up the phone, her first words were, "George, I hope this is you. I've been thinking about you all day."

"Alice, I just bought the old house back. Could we get together this weekend and talk? It's important to me."

"I just happen to be free this weekend, and I don't know anybody I'd rather spend it with than you."

They met.
Love mended.
She stayed.
Forever.

A noble impulse acted upon reunited two people who had allowed the petty things of life to drive them apart. George and Alice Franklin mended their broken relationship and began rebuilding their life together.

Are you burdened with a heavy sense of wrongness? Do you find yourself looking out windows into other people's windows? Have you lost touch with the important people in your life?

God's providential touch may already be working to help you rebuild broken relationships.

Do you need to call somebody?

reflections . . .

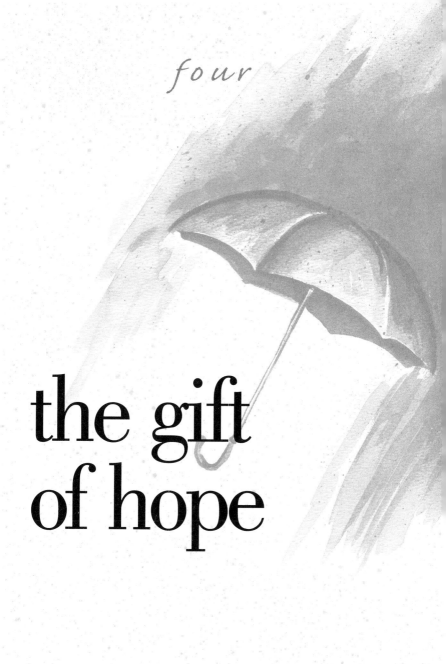

four

the gift
of hope

I love you, and by my amazing grace, I give you never-ending encouragement and good hope. I'm working behind the scenes to encourage your heart and to strengthen you in every good deed and word.

Love,
Your God of All Hope

2 Thessalonians 2:16

Something is wrong – a

regrettable something . . . a heartbreaking something . . . an unexpected and unnerving something. You can't seem to rid yourself of its darkening effect. You've tried to drown it out, drive it away, and push it aside. But it's still with you. Something is wrong.

But there's a solution. There is some*one* right for your some*thing* wrong. He's a healer with a gentle touch, a sympathetic smile, and an intense love. When he speaks, you'll want to listen; when you speak, he hears with an attentive heart. When you see him, you'll notice that he bears deep scars on his hands, his feet, his head, and his side – from a time when things went desperately wrong for him.

In fact, the first things he will want to tell you about are those brutal reminders of something gone wrong.

Don't turn away.

Those ugly mortal wounds hold wonderfully good news for you. They are the key to a *peace* that surpasses pain, to a *confidence* that dispels confusion, to a *hope* that replaces heartbreak.

Run to him, and fall into his embrace.

Jesus has been expecting you – for about 2000 years.

Hope is like the sun,
which, as we journey
toward it, casts the
shadow of our burden
behind us.

—Samuel Smiles

"Oh God," he murmured audibly, *"help me."* And God did.

something's
wrong

It all began because he forgot to turn his car radio on. Those who believe in that sort of thing would call it *providential,* but he did not believe in that sort of thing and would have dismissed it as *circumstantial.*

His wife, Carol, had turned the radio off the evening before because it was news time and her life was depressing enough without the news. Vic always listened to the radio. It was a thirty-minute commute to work, and he passed the time by tapping his fingers on the steering wheel, mouthing a few words, and occasionally even trying to imitate the lead singer. But today – at 6:15 A.M. – he simply forgot to turn it on and consequently fell into an unaccustomed pattern of subconscious thought. Out of that jumbled maze of conflicting future plans and dissatisfaction with past and present ones, a synthesis began to arise. Like a giant air bubble escaping from deep beneath the floor of the ocean where it has lain trapped for centuries, a thought rose with ever increasing speed and burst upon the surface of his consciousness –

something is wrong.

The words were clear, unmistakable. But then they dissipated, leaving only a nagging irritation, like when you don't feel good, but you aren't exactly sick. He reached over quickly and snapped on the radio – a reflexive defense against such unwelcome intrusions – and the thought was lost in the familiar rhythms and lyrics. Well, not exactly lost, but it didn't bother him for many days.

The next time it happened was due to another rare "circumstantial" occurrence. It was the kind of thing that doesn't happen often, but when it does, it is perfectly believable, and the story is told and retold. Only a *very* religious person would have called it providence, and he wasn't even mildly religious. This time, he and Carol had gone to some friends' house for dinner. They were late arriving, and in the hurry and confusion of carrying in the salad and some rolls Carol had made, Vic *accidentally* hit his automatic door lock and locked both his keys and Carol's purse in the car. Their friends had one car in the shop and the other loaned out to a teenage son. Since his house was less than a mile away, Vic decided just to walk home and get his extra set of keys.

A mile is a lot farther than you think when you're alone and it's quiet. There really isn't much to do but think, and he hadn't gone far when the process began. He recognized it, and made several evasive mental moves to block its progress. He walked faster – he concentrated on logistic problems at work – he planned a vacation – but always, behind every maneuver, the process accelerated toward its conclusion. He wished desperately for his telephone, television, radio, even a book or secretary, but nothing came to his aid. He couldn't hold it down. It absolutely burst into consciousness –

Something is wrong!

the gift of hope

And of course something was; in fact, nearly everything was. His job was dissatisfying, yet very demanding. He owed large amounts of money. His marriage was superficial and based more on convenience than love. He had little interest in his children, and they had even less in him. Nothing seemed to taste good anymore, and his laughter was mechanical and heavy. He felt empty – without hope. And one other thing – underneath it all – were those eternal *whys?* His response to the nagging questions had been evasion and philosophy – both of which left him empty and dissatisfied.

He was frantic.

Like the first escaping bubble, so the next thought rose unbidden from so deep within that he could not have identified the place, and the source was totally beyond his reckoning. "Oh God," he murmured audibly, "help me."

And God did.

By *God*, he didn't mean that well-defined, infinite, fully revealed, divine personality known and understood by those whose faith has matured by patiently studying and meditating upon the creation and the Holy Scriptures. He only knew that his problems and questions were greater than himself, and so he used a colloquialism that he had learned both from his childhood and his culture. But that great, eternal Spirit, who in the beginning moved upon the face of the waters and who hovers ever near us, waiting for even the slightest opening, dispatched a messenger to respond.

The message was conveyed to a fellow employee in Vic's department – an underling actually, a rather unobtrusive man whom Vic knew only slightly but whom he had always regarded with some degree of sympathetic disdain because of his lack of drive and business acumen. This employee put a note on Vic's desk two days later, inviting him to a men's Bible study and discussion group at his home. Normally, Vic would have smiled condescendingly and discarded the note. But this time he put it in his pocket, and when the evening came, he went. He was never the same –

and he was glad.

You may not be totally without faith, as Vic was, but you may be haunted by feelings of hopelessness and

the gift of hope

uncertainty. God is working in your life too. His Spirit hovers, ever near, bidding you to seek comfort in the Son. The process of healing will take some time, but you can be confident that hope and assurance are found in him. Open yourself up to his healing –

and *you'll* be glad.

reflections . . . .

the gift of significance

I created you fearfully and wonderfully for significance and purpose! Even before you were conceived, I planned all your days. I'm always watching over you, and I'm familiar with all your ways. Wherever you go, I guide you. My right hand securely holds your precious life.

Love,
Your God of Purpose

Psalm 139

It's a Wonderful Life, with Jimmy Stewart and Donna Reed, is a favorite of young and old alike. Why? Because its message is one that we all long to hear: *Your life is precious!* And it's true, you know. Your life touches the lives of others in a unique, meaningful way – in a way that no other life can. Other people in this world lean on you when they're hurting, want you by their sides when they're celebrating, and need you to listen when they're struggling. A pretty sizable hole would be left if you weren't around.

In the same light, there are people in this world that *you* depend on. How about the friend who wept with you when you faced your greatest loss? Or your mom or dad who showed you that failure is not final and that true love is unconditional.

inspirational message

Or how about the brother or sister with whom you've shared some of your deepest secrets – and they're still secrets.

Sometimes you might allow insecurities and other influences to convince you that your life doesn't matter – that you hold no special significance. But there are nail-scarred hands and an empty grave that proclaim your significance! If you were the only person in the world, Jesus would have walked the same path, shed the same tears, and faced the same brutal death. Why? Because you're _you!_ That's enough for him.

You have been given a great gift – the gift of significance!

No one is useless
to God. No one.

—Max Lucado

When she hung up,
there were great tears
in her eyes, and she
hugged me and
kissed me.

rubber ice

It was late February or early March. James and I were playing at the gravel pit. It was a cold, windy, overcast day, but we were having a great time. I had on my first pair of genuine boots – rubber footwear that you could actually stick your foot right down into with no shoes on – and you didn't have to buckle them. They were black with red soles and a little too big for my feet. (My mother had bought them at a sale, and neither size nor comfort was a major consideration.) Even with two pairs of socks, I "clumped" considerably. They came almost to my knees and looked like firemen's boots.

I was exceedingly proud of them.

There was a little thin ice at the edge of the gravel pit, and we were breaking it by stomping on it and then splashing through into the shallow water beneath.

the gift of significance

I had been doing this for some time when I found a small pool, covered with what we called "rubber ice." It was not actually part of the gravel pit, but it was connected by a narrow neck of water. The ice would actually give with your weight and then spring back – a sort of trampoline effect. You can imagine what fun I had with it. Suddenly, it gave way, and I fell into some sandy water unlike any I had ever been in before. I sank immediately over my boots up to my thighs. Terrified, I began to struggle, but simply could not extricate myself. This produced a fear that resulted in an absolute frenzy of effort to get out. The only noticeable result was that I was nearly up to my armpits within a minute or so.

I did not know that I should remain calm – I simply wore myself out struggling. Finally, I had no energy left, and the absolute futility of further efforts overwhelmed me. James heard my cries and came to help me, but he quickly realized that he could be of no assistance. He stood completely helpless, within ten feet of me. As I grew more calm, I noticed that I wasn't sinking as fast. I told James to run and get Elmer Russell.

rubber ice

He was a well driller, and I knew he was home because I had spoken to him on my way to the gravel pit.

When they returned a few minutes later, I had sunk past my armpits. I was numb from the effect of the freezing sand and water and was quite concerned about my condition. Elmer had brought a rope, and he got a circle of it over my head, and I grabbed it with my hands. Being an extremely powerful man, he pulled me out with relative ease. Unfortunately, he pulled me right out of my boots. It was about a mile or so to my house, but I ran all the way –

in my socks.

I thought I would receive the whipping of my life – but instead, the funniest thing happened. When my mother first saw me – soaking wet, mud and sand right up to my ears, my boots gone – she was real upset. I tried to tell her what had happened, but it was a less than convincing story. Just about the time I finished my explanation, the phone rang, and it was Elmer Russell calling to see if I had gotten home all right. He talked to my mom –

for a long time.

the gift of significance

When she hung up, there were great tears in her eyes, and she hugged me and kissed me. She helped me undress, got the washtub, heated some water, and made me take a hot bath – it wasn't even Saturday – gave me some hot tea, and put me to bed. I couldn't make any sense out of it at all. When my father came home that evening, I thought sure I was going to catch it good.

For some reason, they went to their bedroom to talk, which was really unusual, because normally when I messed up, they talked right in front of me – so I would know what was coming, I guess. I heard her say, "Oh, Fred, Elmer told me that another five minutes and he would have been gone. *We almost lost him.*" When my dad came out, he didn't say much, but I noticed that when we prayed at supper that night, he mentioned me several times and told God how grateful he was that He looked after me when he couldn't.

On Sunday afternoon, he and I walked over to the gravel pit, and I showed him the place – I guess he wanted to look for my boots, but they were nowhere in sight. He stood there by the little pond of water for a long time and looked, and again, he didn't say much;

but I thought I noticed him wiping his eyes a time or two with the back of his hand, and I wondered about it, because the wind was hardly blowing –

and it wasn't that cold.

The lesson is – I know you see it – how the threat of loss makes all that we hold dear more precious – how it moves the love in our hearts. And if the threat of loss moves mere mortals to greater love, how much more does it move our heavenly Father? He sees us struggling frantically to find meaning and purpose in our lives, yet always ending in greater lostness. How pleased he is to circle his great arms around us and rescue us from certain death. And when he carries us home, he says, with great concern, to Jesus and the angelic host –

*"You know,
we almost lost him."*

P.S. Late that fall, I was playing at the gravel pit one sunny afternoon with James (I wasn't real bright as a youngster – some might argue that age hasn't helped substantially), and we found one of my boots sticking

the gift of significance

right up out of the ground. I pulled it out and took it home, but it wasn't much good. I always wondered what happened to the other one.

reflections . . . .

six

the gift of love

*E*ven when your spirit grows faint within you, I know the right and perfect way for you. I'll get you safely through the hidden traps. My endless love for you endures forever! I promise I will never abandon you!

Love,
Your Creator and Faithful Father

Psalm 138:8; 142:3
Deuteronomy 31:6

I have a question

for you. It's not one of those easy, multiple-choice questions, where the answer is provided and all you have to do is guess the right one. No, this is one of those harder questions – it's a fill-in-the-blank. Are you ready?

When times are tough and you feel lost in a sea of sadness, when you feel confused and uncertain of your future, what is the one thing you can absolutely, unquestionably, securely trust? _____

Of course, there are some answers that can easily be ruled out. You know you can't trust your career, money, education, possessions, or the government. When you're really hurting, these are the very things that seem to leave you and let you down the hardest. They are absolutely worthless in bringing comfort or hope. So what's left? Have you filled in the blank yet?

Let me give you a few hints: It's strong enough to move mountains; it's gentle enough to wipe the tear from a child's cheek; it's enduring enough to withstand any crisis; it's healing enough to mend the most broken heart; it's faithful enough to stay when everything else has left or been lost.

It is love – authentic, anchored, life-altering love. It is God's love. Don't waste your time pursuing anything else. Everything else will fail you. Nothing else satisfies, heals, protects, or provides like God's love.

When you call, he comes – he promised he would. When you cry, he tastes salt – he knows your pain. When you can't get up, he lifts you – you are his passion. When you pray for his presence, don't be surprised if you hear a comforting voice in your spirit saying, "I'm already here."

Then, as you lay in the lap of his love, you can look into his eyes and say, "I knew you'd come."

The lengths to which this God will go to express his love for us are almost beyond belief—almost, but not quite.

—Jim McGuiggan

Travis quietly explained his need to go, and even here, in this cold, barren, forbidding setting, the commanding officer realized that there was something unusual here, something not to be treated with normal rules.

i knew
you'd come

I heard this story from George Romney, then Governor of Michigan, in 1955, when I was a junior in high school. It made a deep impression on me, and I have never forgotten it. It is a story about love. I have made up the names, but the rest of the story is told as I remember him telling it.

In the great Ohio Valley, where the fertile, black, loamy soil produces the wheat, corn, potatoes, and other staples for the tables of Detroit and Chicago, there is a small town called Steubenville. It is an old town. Two hundred years ago – and before that – the area was settled by German immigrants who were dissatisfied with life in their native land. What they found there, they liked. They cleared their land; they built

the gift of love

their homes; they established towns, schools, and churches; they had their families – and they stayed.

There is a very old family there named Hansen. It is said that there have always been Hansens in Steubenville. The Hansens are good citizens, close-knit, solid, dependable, courteous, loyal, and helpful. It is a great tribute to the Hansens that whenever a Hansen son or daughter is sent to school, every teacher and administrator is pleased by the prospect.

Some years ago – in the early forties, actually – Lutz Hansen and his wife, Gwendolyn, had two sons in successive years. In fact, they were born eleven months apart. One, the older, they named Travis; the other, James. They had other children – older and eventually younger – but between these two, there developed a closeness, a relationship – a tie – that even in a close-knit family was remarkable – they were inseparable.

Blond, sturdy, intelligent, both were good athletes and good students – and they were always together. They worked, played, even studied together. They were a year apart in school, but with his parent's permission and understanding, Travis stayed out his freshman year of high school so that he and James could play sports together and graduate together. Stories are still told of the way they blocked for each other in football and passed to each other in basketball, how Travis pitched and James caught in baseball, how they always double-dated, and how the girls said it didn't matter which one you went with, because you had a feeling that you were out with both of them.

When they graduated, it was the time of the Korean conflict. They both registered for the draft, and when inducted under the "buddy system," they went to basic training together and later were assigned to the same unit, the same company. They arrived at the Yalu River, north of Panmunjom in January, 1950, in time for a major offensive.

Normally they took their duties together, but one night, James was assigned to a routine perimeter patrol designed to prevent enemy encroachment upon their position. The patrol was ambushed, and only two members struggled back to the camp to report the disaster.

James did not come back.

When word reached Travis, he went immediately to his commanding officer and requested permission to go

the gift of love

and search for his brother. It was denied. The place of the ambush was assumed to be in enemy control, and it would be suicide to send a rescue squad. Travis quietly explained his need to go, and even here, in this cold, barren, forbidding setting, the commanding officer realized that there was something unusual here, something not to be treated with normal rules. He also realized that the boy was going to go – with or without permission.

He finally said that although he could not grant permission, he would not prevent his leaving. Travis spoke to the two men who had made it back, learned the location of the ambush, and set out. It was completely dark; it was unbearably cold; it was a hopeless task; and even if found, his brother had little chance of being alive.

All through that dark night he searched, and just at gray light, he located the place. He moved quickly from one frozen, shattered body to another – not him – not him – and then he found him, nearly frozen, mortally wounded, but alive. He cradled the head of his dying brother in his lap and wept. James opened unseeing eyes, and with the last of his strength whispered –

i knew you'd come

"Is that you, Travis?"
"Yes."
"I knew you'd come –
I've been waiting."

It was the last thing he said. A short time later, he died.

Do things like that really happen? Does love that strong really exist? When Governor Romney told the story, I believed it with all my heart. I want badly to believe it now. Sometimes I need something like this to restore my faith in man's power to do good. Governor Romney didn't say whether or not these boys were religious – I have always believed they were.

James trusted his brother because of the love between them, because love always produces a covenant of trust. He waited because he knew that if the situation were reversed, he would come or die trying. Because of his absolute faith, not just in his brother, but in the power of love itself, he found the strength, had the hope to stay alive – to wait for him to come.

We trust God because he has shown us and taught us love. His love has created a covenant between us and

the gift of love

him. We trust God because we know him and believe that he loves us. We trust each other for the same reason. Because of our absolute faith in God's unfailing, steadfast love, we find the patience and the courage – in the hour of our greatest need – to overcome this world and to wait for him to come.

> When every other reason fails,
> love will find a way.

> "The steadfast love of the Lord never ceases,
> His mercies never come to an end;
> they are new every morning;
> great is your faithfulness.
> 'The Lord is my portion,'
> says my soul,
> 'therefore I will hope in him.'"
> —Lamentations 3:22–23

> "Is that you, Lord?"
> "Yes, John."
> *I knew you'd come –*
> I've been waiting."

reflections . . . .

_____

_____

_____

_____

_____

_____

_____

_____

_____

_____

_____

_____

every good and perfect gift

*D*on't mislabel good things that happen to you as mere "coincidence." See my divine hand in every good and perfect gift that comes your way.

Love,
Your Father of Heavenly Lights

James 1:7

At the moment your pain began, God heard your cry and began to respond. But you must stay alert, or you may mistake the work of the divine healer for mere coincidence.

A knock on your door by a friend, a letter from a loved one, a call from a concerned neighbor, an encouraging word from a family member – all of these are so much more than mere touches of human kindness. In reality, they are gifts from God.

He knows what you're going through. He's intimately familiar with pain. You see, he suffered loss, rejection, failed relationships, and crushing cruelty through the life and death of his only Son.

God's rich compassion is like an endless stream that brings refreshment and renewal to his beloved children. As you yield yourself to his will, he will work his divine providence to refresh and heal your broken heart.

So the next time something or someone comes along "just at the right time" to give comfort or courage, remember that it's more than mere coincidence. The book of James reminds us that "every good gift and perfect gift is from above, coming down from the Father of heavenly lights."

He knows what you need even before you ask – even before you know what to ask for.

God doesn't just patch—
He renews.
God doesn't just salve sins—
He saves.
God doesn't just reform—
He transforms men by
His power.

—Merrill C. Tenney

I went to their rooms –
pinned the notes to
their doors – and left. I
haven't run from many
things in my life– but I
ran from this one.

will he give him a stone?

"Which of you,
if his son asks for bread,
will give him a stone?"
Matthew 7:9

Have you ever received a surprise gift? Something you never would have thought to ask for, something you couldn't possibly plan for. Sometimes these surprise gifts catch you off guard, and if you're not careful, you may not even realize how special they are and so miss much of the blessing.

I took my last two children to Lubbock, Texas, for college. It's a thousand miles from Montgomery to Lubbock. One was a senior, but had never been away from home. The other, a freshman – our baby – the last. The last one is like the first one – but different too. It's a thousand miles from Montgomery to Lubbock.

every good and perfect gift

My excuse for going was that I needed to haul their stuff – which was enough to fill at least one freight car. But it was more than that – I wanted to hang on to them – even for just two or three more days. I was buying time. The inevitable good-bye was a constant oppression.

We arrived Monday afternoon, and they got settled in their rooms. On Tuesday evening, I told them I would pick them up at 8:30 Wednesday morning to help them start registration, then I was going to head home. I couldn't sleep Tuesday night, so I got up and wrote each of them a note. I went in the darkness to their rooms – pinned the notes to their doors – and left. I haven't run from many things in my life – there were many things I should have run from and didn't – but I ran from this one. I just couldn't do it.

Slowly – tearfully, alone – I drove away.

It's forty miles to Post from Lubbock, and before I got there, the sun had begun to rise. It doesn't rain often in West Texas. If you listen to the farmers, it rains like most folks go to church – Christmas and Easter – but it was raining when I left. For those of you not familiar with West Texas, I must explain something. West Texas is *flat*. The most conspicuous, the most striking, the most absolutely mind-boggling, eye-blinking feature of the landscape is its amazing *flatness*. You can see much of the world from West Texas. People who live there think you can see *all* of it. The names of the towns will help you to understand the area. Names like Brown-field, Shallow-water, Post, Little-field, Earth, Plain-view, Level-land, White-face, Ropes-ville, Pan-handle – these are graphic names. The people who originated them were honest, God-fearing folks who wouldn't tell a lie. But back to my story!

Driving to Post, off to my left (to the east), without a single obstruction except for a few oil derricks, was a glorious sunrise – as clear, as totally unclouded as anything you can imagine. Off to my right (to the west), over fields of cotton stretching as far as your imagination will carry you, was a driving rainstorm. In between, ascending in a high arc from north to south, from horizon to horizon, was a rainbow. I want to use some adjectives, I want to say brilliant, spectacular, magnificent – but none of them will do. In fact, it was a double rainbow. One was absolutely clear, with distinct and unmistakable colors; the other, its shadow, was misty and vague. I could see both ends – from ground to ground. I stopped, got out, and just looked. I tried to take pictures, but I couldn't get all of it in the picture frame – not even with a wide-angle lens.

If I could tell you how hope rose in me at the sight of that rainbow – if I could tell you how clearly I felt God's presence – if I could put it into words, I know you would feel it too. I felt as if God, my Father, was laying his hand on my shoulder; I felt as if I heard him say, *"I know how you feel, John. I had to say good-bye to my Son too. It nearly broke my heart. When I saw your pain this morning, I thought you might like this little 'going away' present – from me to you. Lots of other folks will enjoy it, but really, I made it just for you."*

And then it was gone.

One minute it was there – the next it was gone – without a trace. But it will live in my heart and mind forever.

What an insight into the nature of divine fatherhood, and what an example for earthly fathers.

will he give him a stone?

My children awoke that morning fully expecting me to be there; instead they found notes. I believe that my absence conveyed more than my presence could have. I believe that my simple note of love and understanding communicated in a far more lasting way my feeling for them. God responded to my prayers with a totally unexpected token of love and assurance. I had prayed for strength, for faith, and assurance – and he answered my prayer in the shape of a rainbow.

I wonder how many times I have asked for healing and missed the medicine. I wonder how many times I have pouted and doubted because I thought he didn't care, when the problem was with my eyes, my ears, my heart.

> "If you, then, though you are evil,
> know how to give good gifts to your children,
> how much more will your Father in heaven
> give good things to those who ask him!"
> —Matthew 7:11

reflections . . .